GIAN CARLO MENOTTI

THE OLD MAID AND THE THIEF

A Grotesque Opera

in 14 scenes

———

VOCAL SCORE

—

F.C. 1282

GIAN-CARLO MENOTTI

THE OLD MAID AND THE THIEF

———

CHARACTERS

MISS TODD ....Contralto

LAETITIA ... .,.... Soprano

MISS PINKERTON.................,....,.... Soprano

BOB..........................,..... . ...,..... Baritone

———

The Action Takes Place in a Small Town. Somewhere in the United States.

Time: The Present.

———

"The Old Maid and the Thief" was originally conceived as a Radio-Opera and Broadcast as World Premiere by the National Broadcasting Company, April 22, 1939.
First stage performance by the Philadelphia Opera Company,
February 11, 1941

THE OLD MAID AND THE THIEF

ANNOUNCEMENTS BEFORE EACH SCENE
(For Radio presentation only)

Announcer:

SCENE 1

It is late afternoon in Miss Todd's parlor. A visitor is just arriving.

SCENE 2

The next morning Laetitia is busy with her pots and pans when Miss Todd comes into the kitchen.

SCENE 3

Bob's breakfast is ready and Laetitia proudly carries the heaping tray into the guest room where Bob lies drowsily in bed.

SCENE 4

A few minutes later Miss Todd ventures out of the house, to do some marketing. Down the block whom does she see approaching, but her friend, Miss Pinkerton.

SCENE 5

Miss Todd can't hurry home quickly enough, for the similarity of Bob's appearance and the description Miss Pinkerton gave of the escaped criminal has given her plenty of cause for alarm. Into the front door she flies and into the parlor where Laetitia is dusting.

SCENE 6

The days pass by. Bob remains a guest in Miss Todd's house. A week later we find Laetitia in the kitchen taking pains mending and then pressing a pair of well-worn trousers, Bob's, of course!

SCENE 7

A little later in the day Miss Todd is sitting on her front porch when Miss Pinkerton rushes up the steps in breathless excitement.

SCENE 8 and 9

A few days go by. Miss Todd is sitting in her parlor. Laetitia is in the kitchen getting ready to go upstairs with the customary morning tray, so that Bob can have his breakfast in bed as usual. Meanwhile Bob, up in his room, prompted by a desire to take to the road again is secretly making a bundle of his clothes.

SCENE 10

Two o'clock in the morning. The village is sleeping quietly. In front of the liquor store all is deserted, but down the block two stealthy figures are approaching.

SCENE 11

The next morning Miss Todd is in her parlor when the door burst open.

SCENE 12 and 13

Hurry, Miss Todd! Hurry, Laetitia! There is no time to lose! Out of the parlor, up the stairs to Bob's room. But they find the door closed.

SCENE 14

A few minutes later Miss Todd returns to her house . . . and this, ladies and gentlemen, is the final scene.

To my Mother

THE OLD MAID AND THE THIEF
Overture

Text and Music by
GIAN CARLO MENOTTI

Presto, con brio (♩ = 176)

F.C. 1282

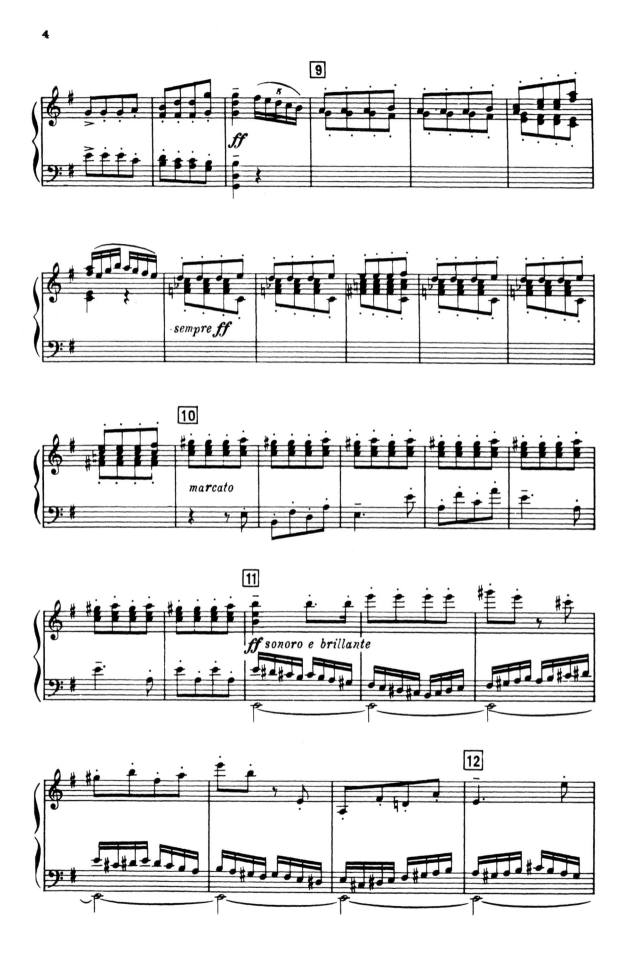

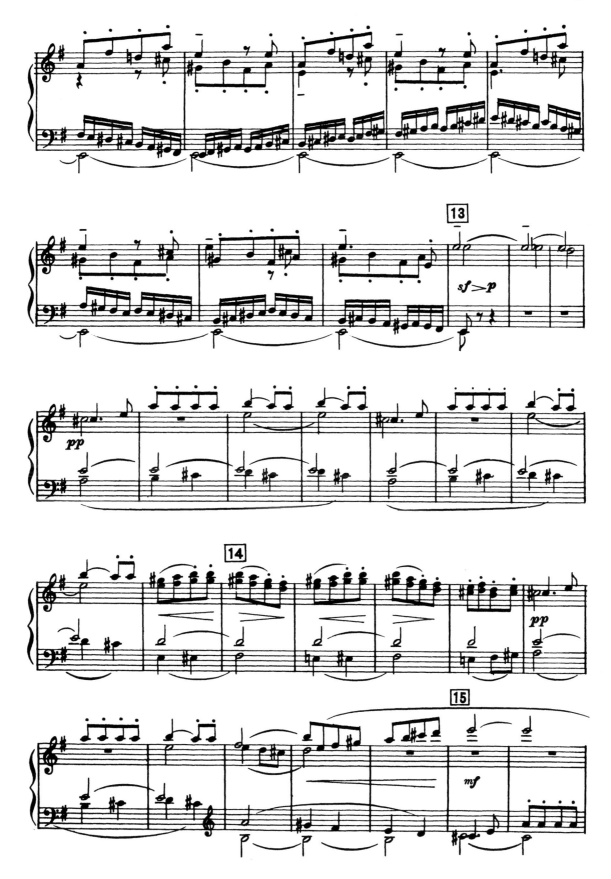

ff
ben marcato

8

12

(N.B. The opera must be staged in such a way that no curtain or pause is required between one scene and the next)

SCENE I:- In Miss Todd's Parlor
(Late Afternoon)

14

MISS PINKERTON

Miss Todd good day.

MISS TODD

Good day, Miss Pin-ker-ton.

Give me your man-te-let, your

o-ver-shoes.

Make your-self

M.P.

Don't

M.T.

com - for - ta - ble and tell me the news while I make some tea.

espr.

M.P.

trou - ble your - self for me!

3

M.T.

No trou - ble at all. The

p

M.P.

M.T.

wa - ter is boil - ing in the ket - tle...

p   *p*

16

on which to fix his mast he sailed for his first

all this time he took to read and read _____

trip _____ that's when I saw him last.___ Life is

for all this time he took to read and read.___ Life is

but a bro-ken prom-ise. And why should God keep his

but a bro-ken prom-ise. And why should God keep his

26

28

40

SCENE II:- The Kitchen of Miss Todd's House

Next Morning

The church bell strikes eight o'clock. Lights

Allegro, molto mosso

LAETITIA *(preparing a breakfast tray)*

MISS TODD   *(appearing in her kimono)*

Good day, Lae-

L.

Good morn-ing, mad-ame! Why up so ear-ly?

M.T.

ti - tia.

L.

M.T.

All night I felt so ex-cit-ed, I could not sleep a

L.

I am in no po-

M.T.

But who shall make him the prop-o-si-tion? I do not dare.

38

p

si-tion.

L.

I think you'd bet-ter.

What both-er-a-tion!

It's your af-fair.

M.T.

I'll write a let-ter.

poco rit.

f

poco meno mosso

L.

If you don't dare to face the mat-ter

L. poco rall.

I shall take care of it with a good breakfast.

poco meno mosso

f marcato

p poco rall.

(Proudly carrying her breakfast tray and humming to herself Laetitia goes upstairs)

(liberamente)

40

L.

tr tr tr

Ah!

a tempo

SCENE III:- Bob's Bedroom
(Immediately after)

SCENE IV:- In the Street
(Immediately after)

Presto agitato

MISS PINKERTON

Miss Todd!_____ Miss

MISS TODD

M.P.

Todd!_____

M.T.

Miss Pin-ker-ton, good

M.P. (waving a newspaper)

Have you heard! Have you

M.T.

morn - ing

64

read!   A most ter - ri - ble thief has

fled   from the coun - ty jail of Tim - ber-ville. The

town is in great fear   for he was seen not far from

Keep all the win - dows closed! He has com-mit - ted
crime af-ter crime for as lit - tle as a dime.
Keep all the doors locked! Keep all the

SCENE V:- Miss Todd's Parlor
(Immediately after)

74 66

tressed who told me a thief has fled from the

coun - ty jail of Tim - ber-ville. A thief, a mur-der-er, she

said! He was seen not far from here; and, my dear, he's

L.

M.T.
here? Al-ready I've made Miss Pin-ker - ton be-lieve that he is my

mp

L.

73

M.T.
cou - sin Steve. We must be great tac - ti - cians and

mf

mf

L.

M.T.
rid our-selves of him in a more sub-tle way as

p

sf

sf

There is no al-ter-na-tive, we'll have to keep him here.

Why! Lae-ti-tia! You must be out of your mind! A

la-dy of my kind to en-ter-tain a fu-gi-tive! He'll rob and

82

88

89 L.

no one shall ev - er know of it, no one shall ev - er know of it.

M.T.

Your

p subito

L.

M.T.

ar - gu-ment is weak,_____ but so am I._____

90

L.

I don't see what is wrong with it. The

M.T.

espr.

mp

SCENE *VI*:- The Kitchen
(A Week Later)

The church bell strikes four o'clock. Lights

Larghetto

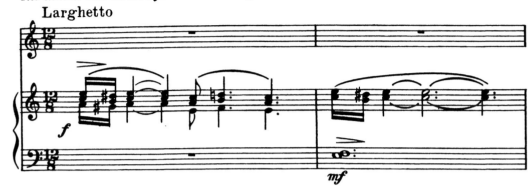

LAETITIA *(Alone, mending Bob's trousers)*

What a curse for a wo-man is a tim-id man! A

L.

week has gone by; he had plen-ty of chanc - es,

94

L.

poco più mosso

but he made no ad-van - ces. Miss Todd schemes and lab-ors to

L. *(She gets up and busies herself with iron and ironing board)*

All the drawers are wide op - en, all the doors are un-locked .. He

96
(With disgust)

L. neith - er seems pleased nor shocked. He eats and drinks and

L. sleeps, he talks of base-ball and box - ing... but

L. that is all. What a curse for a wo-man is a tim-id man!

SCENE VII:- In Miss Todd's Parlor
(Immediately after)

M. P.

Miss Pax - son has not seen her purse since that

M. T.

M. P.
rall.
a tempo

morn- ing you came for a vi - sit.

M. T.

There is no more doubt the

108

p *rall.* *mf* *a tempo*

M. P.

And since our church meet- ing on Mon- day the

M. T.

rob- ber must be here - a - bout!

mf

Poco meno mosso

M.P.
Sun - day col - lec - tion is miss-ing. We must ask the po - lice for pro-

M.T.
We must ask the po - lice for pro-

Poco meno mosso [108]

M.P.
tec-tion we must, we must.

M.T.
tec-tion we must, we must.

(Suddenly, in complete silence, Laetitia cross-es the room proudly carrying over her arms Bob's freshly pressed trousers—Miss Pinkerton stares openmouthed, while Laetitia mounts the stairs and hands the trousers to Bob through the bed-room door opened to a crack)

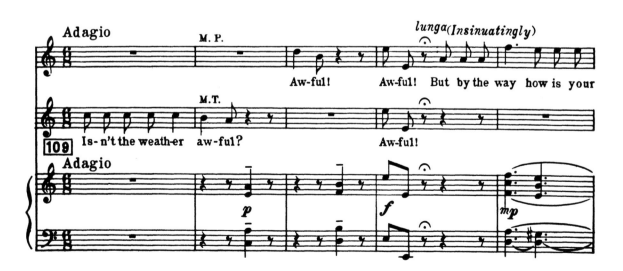

Adagio

M.P.
lunga (Insinuatingly)
Aw-ful! Aw-ful! But by the way how is your

M.T.
[109] Is- n't the weath-er aw-ful? Aw-ful!

Adagio

SCENE *VIII*:- Bob's Bedroom
(Immediately after)

(Bob has finished dressing and now begins making his bundle)

Andante calmo, ma senza trascinare

When the air sings of sum-mer, I must

wan-der a-gain. Sweet land-lord is the sky, rich house is the plain,

and to live is to wan-der through the sun and the rain.

When the air sings of sum-mer I must wan-der a - gain.____

First you wan - der in youth and joy   then you'll wan - der to still the fears

in an old heart   First you wan - der to find your love,

then you'll wan - der to hide your tears,   for a wand'-rer must de-part.

When a man owns a house he is a bird in a cage whose cap-tiv-i-ty pain

is sweet-en'd with age. Ah! the sharp joy of free-dom

is my loss and my gain. When the air sings of sum-mer I must

wan-der a-gain.

106

Allegro ma non troppo

LAETITIA *(Laetitia is seen going upstairs with a tea tray)*

BOB

L.

B.

be - ing shut in a house all day long makes me rest - less ner-vous and weak.

L.
(*Supplicatingly*)

Please, dear Bob, don't go a-way! If you stay an - oth - er week

B.

117

Poco meno mosso

a tempo

ff

mf

L.

118

we'll give you more mon - ey.

We're

B.

This is not what I seek.

mf

110

SCENE IX:- The Parlor
(Immediately Afterwards)

L.

M.T. (liberamente)

It might be for the best. This clear-ly shows that for me he has

mp *p*

L. (Insinuatingly)

His braz-en re-quest

M.T.

no use.

mf

L.

might be on-ly an ex-cuse to put your love to the test.

M.T.

mf *mf*

116

SCENE X:- In Front of the Liquor Store
(That Same Night)

Allegro moderato
Bell in B

(A policeman is seen crossing the stage.

As soon as he disappears around the corner, Laetitia and Miss Todd make their entrance

carrying flashlights)

LAETITIA

Look to your left.

MISS TODD

Look to your right.

(scanning the audience with their

(A whole pile of bottles crashes to the floor with a frightful racket)

Un poco più

You sil - ly fool! What have you done!

(The voice of the storekeeper is heard from upstairs saying: "Who's there!")

(Policeman re-enters. Stares

incredulously at the wrecked store)

SCENE XI:- Miss Todd's Parlor
(The Next Morning)

(Miss Todd is seen sitting demurely, busy at her knitting)

FC 1282

136

SCENE XII:- Bob's Bedroom
(Immediately Afterwards)

140

144

148

156

clear. I'll tell them my tale; jus - tice won't fail.

Well, young man, you ask for your doom.

MISS TODD ... *(Spoken)* Laetitia don't let him get out of this room! I'll go and call the
201 police.

Tempo di walzer

(Miss Todd exit)

SCENE XIII:- The Same
(Immediately Afterwards)

Adagio ma non troppo
(Laetitia sits next to Bob and coquettishly lays her head on his shoulder)

168

170

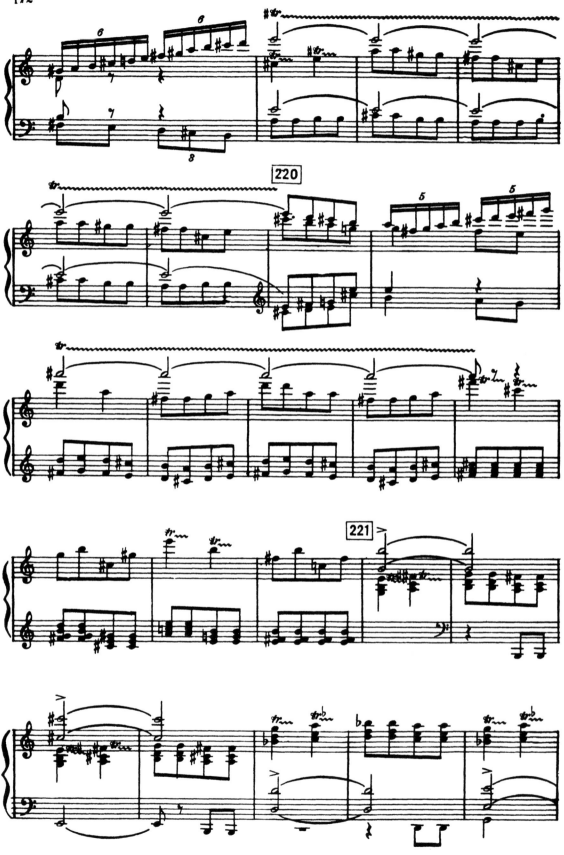

225 (They are seen driving away on the loaded

car)

SCENE XIV:- Miss Todd's Parlor

M. T.

strange-ly si-lent the house! ... Lae-ti - tia!_____ Lae-ti-

M. T.

(She goes upstairs to Bob's room)

- tia!_____

229

M. T.

How odd! The room is emp-ty! Lae-ti - tia!

M. T.

Bob! I was just jok-ing...

231

M. T.

They have run off to-geth-er! They have ransacked and plun-dered my

cresc. - - - - - - - -

M. T.

house! They have ev-en stol-en my car!

ff

232

M. T.

Help!__ Help!__ Help!__ Thieves!

ff

M. T.

__ Thieves! They have stol-en my sil-ver!

Help!

(She falls fainting into her chair, holding in her hand an empty liquor bottle Bob has left behind)

Help!

235

(Miss Pinkerton knocks at the door, then peeks in. She views the scene with triumphant

indignation)

(Curtain)